THE
VERY BUSY

LETTER
Y

PHONICS READ-ALOUDS

Title: The Very Busy Letter Y
ISBN: 9798339438076
First Published in the United States of America, 2024

Contributors: Manns, Yvette, author; Blu, Ana K., illustrator

Summary: Y feels left out because there aren't that many words that start with the letter Y. She goes undercover as a spy and works as a vowel in words that have a Y in the middle and at the end.

THE
VERY TALENTED
LETTER Y

Written by: Yvette Manns
Illustrated by: Ana K. Blu

The letter Y loved to stay busy.

In the morning, she did yoga at sunrise.

At noon, she read a story while eating yogurt for lunch.

At night, she practiced knitting with yarn before bed.

Even after all those daily activities, Y was still bored! Y figured her consonant friends were probably building words with the vowels. She considered looking for her friend, S.

Y found S near Vowel Valley while S was on the search for E.

"Hey, Y," S said. "Would you like to build a word with us?"

"You bet!" Y answered.

The letters lined up to build the word "yes."

"That was so much fun!" Y yelled. "Sometimes I wish I could be in more words, especially like you, E."

E smiled, "Maybe one day you will."

On the way home, Y saw a yellow building she never noticed before. There was a sign in the window that caught her eye.

Y went inside to apply for a job. She was greeted by a familiar face - her friend X.

X said, "I'm Agent X. Let's begin your journey as a secret spy."

Y was so excited! She left Agent X's office and tiptoed through Vowel Valley. She had to be very sneaky to pry for information about the sounds these letters represent. This would help Y on her spy missions.

When Y got home, she stayed up all night to study for her spy exam. Y was ready to ace her test with Agent X.

Y's hard work paid off, and she passed her test with flying colors. Agent X gave Y a shiny spy badge and a red hat so she would blend in with the red vowel letters. Y was ready to begin her undercover missions working as a vowel.

Mission One: Y as Long E

The first mission was to stand in for E's long sound at the end of words with two syllables. Y jumped in as a happy girl was eating candy.

happy

candy

Mission Two: Y as Long I

Y's second mission was to replace I's long sound at the end of one-syllable words. Y spotted another spy flying overhead in the sky.

Y continued this mission with words that had a Y between two consonants. She replaced I's long sound in words with a consonant, Y, another consonant, then silent E.

type

rhyme

Mission Three: Y as Short I

Y's third mission was to step in for I's short sound in the middle of words and syllables. She entered a gym and saw cheerleaders forming a pyramid with band members playing the cymbals.

gym

pyramid

cymbals

Y was sleepy after a long day of completing spy missions. She marched over to Agent X's office.

"Why didn't you tell me these spy missions were so much work?" Y asked. "Being a vowel sound isn't easy at all!"

Agent X replied, "What was so tricky about your missions?"

"I didn't know I would have so many different sounds as a vowel!" Y answered as she gave Agent X an icy glare.

X explained, "A good spy works hard, hides their identity, remembers the rules to decode, and knows there are exceptions to the rules. It's as easy as pie."

Y yelled, "Well, I don't want to be a spy anymore! I quit!"

As Y headed home, she heard her name being called. "Hey, Y! We know you went undercover and took some of our sounds today," E said.

I continued, "Since you did most of my work today, why don't I help you sometimes? I'll take your consonant sound in words like 'onion' and 'brilliant.' Deal?"

"Deal," Y answered.

A, E, I, O, U, and Y celebrated her new job as a vowel sound.

Suddenly, Y noticed X behind a bush nearby.

X said, "So, Y, now that you are no longer a spy, which sounds are you giving up - your new vowel sounds or your consonant sound?"

Y replied, "I will keep the /y/ sound at the beginning of words and syllables that begin with Y. I will borrow E's long sound, I's short sound, and I's long sound in the word patterns I learned from my spy missions if that's okay with the vowels."

The vowels replied, "That sounds great to us!"

"Well, Y," X said, "You wanted to be more involved in words because your consonant sound wasn't that common. Now, working as a vowel, you will have even more ways to stay busy. What do you think about that?"

"YAHOO!

Y yelled.

TIPS FOR AFTER READING

- Go on a word hunt and list all the words in this story with Y as a vowel.
- Categorize the words you find by the sound Y represents in the words and share with a classmate.
- Read all the words with Y as a vowel sound out loud.
- Using another passage or text, highlight all the words you can find that have Y as a vowel.
- Look for words that have a letter Y in them, and the Y is representing its consonant sound.

FUN FACTS ABOUT
Y AS A VOWEL SOUND

- The written letter Y can represent four sounds in English - its consonant sound, long E, long I and short I.
- Y is a vowel at the end of a word.
- The letter Y also works as a suffix that describes the noun it is attached to.
- Y represents a vowel sound more often than it represents a consonant sound.
- The most common sound that Y represents is long E at the end of a word.
- When some words have two syllables and end with the letters F, L, or N, the Y sounds like long I instead of long E. For example: deny, apply, rely.
- The least common sound that Y represents is its consonant sound.
- Here are some more words that have Y as a vowel:

> angry apply bye cycle deny dry gym hazy
> identity lazy myth navy pony reply symbol tidy

CAN YOU THINK OF ANY MORE WORDS WITH
Y AS A VOWEL SOUND?

CHECK OUT OTHER BOOKS IN THE SERIES!

...and more books!

STAY IN THE KNOW!

Visit
www.PhonicsReadAlouds.com
for activities, stickers and more!

DID YOU ENJOY THIS STORY?

⭐⭐⭐⭐⭐

Please consider leaving us a review on Amazon. This helps us to learn what you want to read about next and tell other people about our stories!

Made in United States
Orlando, FL
16 November 2024